Weird Science

Look for other

titles:
World's Weirdest Critters
Creepy Stuff
Odd-inary People
Amazing Escapes
World's Weirdest Gadgets
Bizarre Bugs
Blasts from the Past
Awesome Animals

Weird
Science

by Mary Packard

and the Editors of Ripley Entertainment Inc.

illustrations by Leanne Franson

SCHOLASTIC INC.

New York   Toronto   London   Auckland   Sydney
Mexico City   New Delhi   Hong Kong   Buenos Aires

Developed by Nancy Hall, Inc.
Designed by R studio T
Cover design by Atif Toor
Photo research by Laura Miller

ISBN 0-439-56421-2

12 11 10 9 8 7 6 5 4 3 2 1   3 4 5 6 7 8/0

Printed in the U.S.A.
First printing, November 2003

40

Contents

Weird
Science

Introduction

Reach for the Stars

The great Robert Ripley, creator of Believe It or Not!, was the first millionaire cartoonist in history. A man of many talents, he was an athlete, artist, writer, showman, and businessman all rolled into one. In the 1930s and '40s, at the height of his career, there was almost no one who had not heard of him. And whenever anything unusual

happened, "There's one for Rip!" was the phrase that would most often spring to people's lips.

Though Ripley had a passion for the bizarre, he was well aware that what gave each Believe It or Not! cartoon its spine-tingling quality was the fact that it was true. It's no wonder then that science was such a natural source of material for him.

When asked, "Where do you get all your facts?" Ripley would reply, "Everywhere and all the time. It's impossible to run dry on astonishing facts about the world." He considered scientists to be among the most fascinating people on Earth. After all, they shared his wonder at the world, always looking for fresh ways to investigate common everyday phenomena.

For Ripley, learning how the world worked was a labor of love. The fact that a mouse has more bones

than a person and that there are a hundred times more species of insects than visible stars on a clear night filled him with delight. Blue moons, colossal vegetables, frozen waterfalls, arboreal lightning, shooting stars—these scientific subjects inspired some of Ripley's most successful cartoons.

A world-class traveler, Robert Ripley was one of the few people to have visited more than 200 countries during his lifetime. Each of Ripley's excursions contributed new and awesome wonders to enliven his cartoons and enrich his treasure trove of unbelievable facts. Through the wonders of science, Ripley was able to expand the boundaries of his mind as well.

Had Ripley lived to see the 21st century, imagine what he would have thought of the amazing new discoveries that are being made in science and technology—space stations, genetic engineering, slug-eating robots. It boggles the mind!

Weird Science is packed with surprising scientific facts and mind-stretching new research. See how much you already know by taking the That's Wild! quizzes and the Ripley's Brain Buster in each chapter. Then go on to the Pop Quiz at the end of the book and figure out your Ripley's rank with the handy scorecard.

Remember, for Robert Ripley, the sky was the limit, and you can reach for the stars!

Believe It!®

Many odd experiments result in useful information that enriches our lives— but a lot of other scientific research is just plain goofy.

Milky Way: Do cows like music? Researchers at England's University of Leicester piped different kinds of music into a dairy barn holding 1,000 cows. Playing Simon and Garfunkel's "Bridge Over Troubled Water" resulted in a three-percent rise in milk production. However, when faster, louder music was played, production remained the same, proving that cows do like some kinds of music better than others!

That's Wild!

Researchers at Ohio State University have discovered that cows digest their food better after . . .

a. ground-up Tums are mixed into their food.
b. they swallow plastic pot scrubbers.
c. they were given a massage.
d. they had fruit for dessert.

Tuning Out: A group of unruly teenagers were hanging out at a commuter train station in Boston, causing fights and creating disturbances. Arresting the kids didn't work. They just kept coming back. So officials of the Massachusetts Bay Transportation Authority tried an experiment. They piped light classical music throughout the station. The teens took off in a flash, and so far, they haven't returned!

Just Spit It Out! Carl J. Charnetski and Francis Brennan, Jr., researchers at Wilkes University in Pennsylvania, had people listen to different types of music. After each selection, they were asked to spit so the researchers could measure the amount of the virus-fighting immunoglobulin A (IgA) in their saliva. The results indicated that more IgA was found in the saliva of people who had just listened to elevator music. Does this mean elevator music can keep you from getting a cold? The researchers seem to think so.

That's Wild!

Researchers at the University of Michigan believe that chocolate can be used to make . . .

a. glue.
b. diesel fuel.
c. shock absorbers for cars.
d. suntan lotion.

A Real Stinker: United States researchers are developing an odor bomb. The military hopes to use it to clear people out of public places without harming them. To create the most odoriferous bomb, they are experimenting with a vast array of smelly stuff, such as human waste, vomit, garbage, and burned hair. Wouldn't you like to work in that lab?

What a Gas! Researcher Buck Weimer of Pueblo, Colorado, spent several years performing experiments

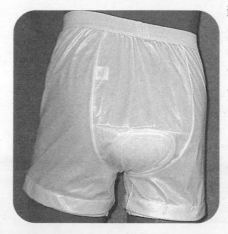

in an effort to develop a product that would filter out bad smells. He came up with Under-Ease, underwear with a charcoal filter that will remove stinky gases before they escape into the air. Under-Ease is available for both men and women—and the filter can be replaced.

Flights of Fancy: Why would people dress up in whooping crane costumes? Because they're raising young cranes and don't want the birds to get used to humans. The cranes are being raised in an effort to establish a new migrating flock. There are only about 200 whooping cranes in the wild and only one flock that migrates. The new flock will fly from Wisconsin to Florida. Along the way, the cranes can rest in wildlife refuges and in the fields of friendly farmers where they will be safe. How do they learn the route? By following an ultralight airplane flown by a costumed pilot.

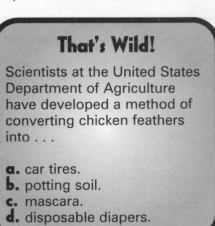

That's Wild!

Scientists at the United States Department of Agriculture have developed a method of converting chicken feathers into . . .

a. car tires.
b. potting soil.
c. mascara.
d. disposable diapers.

Sticky Problem: Geckos are those little lizards that seem to defy gravity when they scurry up walls and across ceilings. A few scientists decided to figure out how they do it. They found out that gecko feet are coated with millions of tiny hairs. Weak electric charges in the hairs and on

the surfaces they climb create a kind of static cling and keep them from falling. What do the researchers plan to do with their findings? Would you believe that they hope to create wall-climbing robots?

Jump Start: On September 7, 2001, British children from 5,000 schools took part in a scientific experiment. One million children jumped up and down for a full minute, from 11:00 A.M. to 11:01 A.M., in hopes of creating a measurable earthquake. Did it work? According to local seismometers, the "giant jump" generated 1/100th of an average earthquake. It also set a world record for the largest simultaneous jump.

Shower Power: Ever wonder why the shower curtain blows in at you when you take a hot shower? A researcher at the University of Massachusetts took it upon himself to solve the mystery once and for all. Using computer software developed by Fluent, Inc., David Schmidt demonstrated that the force that sucks a shower curtain inward is created by low pressure on the inside of the shower curtain and high pressure on the outside. On the computer, the circulating low-pressure air inside the shower looks a lot like a satellite photo of a hurricane.

Look Ma, No Brains!

Scientists in Naboya, Japan, have determined that slime mold, a single-cell, brainless organism, can change its shape and make its way through a maze to get food.

That's Wild!

Felix Wäckers, a biologist at the Netherlands Institute of Ecology, has distinguished himself by training these creatures to detect drugs and bombs.

a. Capuchin monkeys
b. Raccoons
c. Dolphins
d. Wasps

Wet Test: As a result of their research, meteorologists Trevor Wallis and Thomas Peterson of the National Climatic Data Center in Asheville, North Carolina, were able to say with certainty that a person walking in the rain would get 40 percent wetter than a person who runs.

Of Mites and Men: Dr. Robert A. Lopez of Westport, New York, is one veterinarian who has gone beyond the call of duty in the name of research. He extracted ear

mites from cats and planted them in his own ear! Lopez treated himself, and after his ear healed, he repeated the experiment two more times. His findings? As they scurry around the ear canal, the host can both feel and hear the annoying little critters.

Talking Trash: Scientists at the University of Arizona have dug up some interesting facts about garbage. One finding is that newspapers take up a great deal of space in landfills. Many newspapers are still readable even after they've been

buried for 20 or 30 years. And researchers are not quite sure what to make of this: After Halloween, there are a lot of candy wrappers and not much candy, but after Valentine's Day, the reverse is true.

Butter Fingers: British physicist Robert Matthews conducted an experiment in which 1,000 schoolchildren

dropped nearly 10,000 pieces of buttered toast onto the floor. The results confirmed his theory that Murphy's Law (anything that can go wrong will go wrong) would prevail. The bread landed on the buttered side 62 percent of the time.

Seeds of Learning:

A team of scientists at Keio University in Japan set out to see if pigeons can tell the paintings of one artist from another. The birds were shown slides in random order. Half the group

was fed seeds every time it saw a Monet painting. The other half was given seeds when it saw a painting by Picasso. After three weeks, the birds were tested. Most achieved a score of 90 percent on the test. Not bad for a class of birdbrains!

Long Shot:

When researchers at Whiteshell Nuclear Research Establishment in Pinawa, Manitoba, Canada, injected golf balls with 300 kilorads of radiation, the nuked balls bounced from three to eight percent higher than ordinary golf balls. To spread the word, the laboratory invited people to send in their golf balls for a complimentary zapping to increase their range. In one year, they received about 7,000 golf balls sent by people from all over the world.

That's Wild!

Professor Jean-Marc Vanden-Broeck of the University of East Anglia in Norwich, England, has spent 17 years researching a method of making . . .

a. a teapot spout that won't drip.
b. sunscreen from the vanilla bean.
c. a car that runs on onion dip.
d. sugar out of sand.

A Tad Disgusting:

Brightly colored tadpoles are easy for predators to spot. So biologist Richard Wassersug reasoned that they must taste bad, too, otherwise none would survive to become frogs. To test his theory, he and his graduate students went on a field trip to Costa Rica, and—you guessed it—the students tasted a variety of raw tadpoles. The results? The brightly colored tadpoles were the yuckiest-tasting of the bunch.

Making Waves:

Have you ever watched a sports event and seen the "wave" made by sitting fans standing up, then sitting down again? To find out more about these waves, physicists in Hungary built a computer model of one. Their findings? A wave usually travels

clockwise at about 20 seats per second, and at least 40 people are needed to create one.

Really Bad Breath:

Carbon dioxide from methane gas and burning fossil fuels trap the sun's heat close to Earth, causing global warming. Cows produce a lot of methane, which they release in the form of burps—every 40 seconds! To find out if changing a cow's diet would cause it to release a less harmful form of gas, scientist Patrick Zimmerman designed a burp trap—a container that hangs around a cow's neck and has a tube leading to its mouth. If he's right, changing what the cows eat might improve the climate. Now, if they could only teach the cows to say "Excuse me!"

Slam Dunk:

With the help of such scientific instruments as a belt sander, an X-ray machine, scales, and a microscope, physicist Len Fisher of the University of Bristol in England was able to calculate the best way to dunk a cookie. His conclusions? Different cookies have different optimal dunking times, and cookies covered with chocolate on one side should be dipped with the chocolate side up.

That's Wild!

Norwegian marine biologist Erlend Moksness has conducted research that proves that fish . . .

a. can get seasick.
b. mate for life.
c. can change their gender.
d. smell with their fins.

Pooper Scoopers:

Some people think luak coffee from Indonesia is the best-tasting coffee there is. Why does it taste so good? The luak, a small, dark-brown relative of the bobcat, likes to eat the fruit of the best coffee plants. It digests the sticky outer husk of the fruit, but not the beans. To harvest the beans, people simply gather up the piles of poop left by the luak. The trip through the animal's digestive system seems to improve the coffee! One might wonder what prompted this avenue of research, but it has certainly paid off. Luak coffee is the most expensive blend in the entire world.

That's Wild!

United States scientists drilled 396 feet into the snow at the South Pole in order to get samples of air that is . . .

a. 1,000 years old.
b. 500 years old.
c. 100 years old.
d. 10,000 years old.

Brain Buster

Time to experiment! See how you measure up by testing your ability to tell the difference between freaky facts and far-out fictions.

Robert Ripley dedicated his life to seeking out the bizarre and unusual. But every unbelievable thing he recorded was known to be true. In the Brain Busters at the end of every chapter, you'll play Ripley's role—trying to verify the fantastic facts presented. Each Ripley's Brain Buster contains a group of four shocking statements. But of these so-called "facts," **one** is **fiction**. Will you **Believe It!** or **Not!**?

Wait—there's more! Following the Brain Busters are special bonus games called "What's the Wonder?" where you can earn extra points! Keep score by flipping to the end of the book for answer keys and a scorecard.

Science experiments can be complicated and take many years of research. Or they can be simple and fun! Below are four experiments and creations you can try in your very own home. But one of them just doesn't add up. Can you pick out the fake?

a. With the right equipment, you can make a battery out of a potato.

Believe It! **Not!**

17

b. Elmer's Glue, borax, water, and some food coloring are all you need to make your very own slime!

Believe It!   Not!

c. A piece of paper taped into a funnel shape can be used as a hearing aid.

Believe It!   Not!

d. Experiment with different flavors of chewing gum by combining honey, sugar, water, and fruit!

Believe It!   Not!

• •

BONUS GAME
What's the Wonder?

A popular project for school science fairs involves creating a fake volcano that actually "erupts." The lava is usually a combination of baking soda and water (and some red food coloring), which, when put together, cause a very cool chemical reaction. The baking soda and water form a certain gas that pushes the lava up and out the volcano top. Can you name the gas? What is this wonder that causes volcanic eruptions?

C _ _ _ _   D _ _ _ _ _ _

Here are some things you might like to know about the human body—and some you might prefer *not* to know!

Sum of Its Parts:

The human body has a net worth of about $4.50! That's the monetary value of its elements—including oxygen, carbon, hydrogen, and calcium.

That's Wild!

In 75 years, the human heart pumps enough blood to fill . . .

a. the Grand Canyon.
b. a hotel-sized swimming pool 20 times.
c. a Boeing 707 airplane.
d. an oil tanker more than 46 times.

Have a Heart: After people have heart attacks, injured cells are replaced by scar tissue, resulting in heart damage. Researchers at Harvard University are hoping that by studying zebrafish, they will learn how to restore human hearts. The research team anesthetized ten zebrafish, then cut away 20 percent of the heart tissue. They returned the eight fish that survived to the water. Within ten days, the fish were swimming normally, and within two months, all the lost heart tissue had grown back!

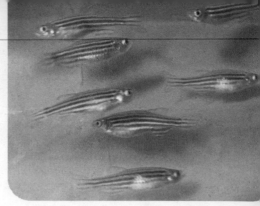

Breaking the Code: Deoxyribonucleic acid (DNA) is a molecule that looks like a spiral-shaped ladder and contains our genes. In 2000, after ten years of trying, scientists working in labs all over the world managed to string together all three billion rungs of the DNA ladder in the correct order! Only about five percent of DNA is made up of genes. But pinpointing the function of each one can help scientists find the causes of many serious diseases. Amazingly, just a small change in the order of the gene sequence can spell the difference between sickness and health!

Chew on This! A scientist at England's University of Northumbria gave 75 people a 25-minute memory test. Some chewed gum, some did not, and the rest just pretended to chew. The real gum chewers scored a lot higher than the rest. Why? It's possible that chewing gum makes the heart beat faster, pumping more oxygen to the brain and improving memory.

Gesundheit! Can you guess what Autosomal Dominant Compelling Helio-Opthalmic Outburst syndrome describes? It's a fancy name for people who sneeze when exposed to bright light. Its acronym is ACHOO, and up to 30 percent of the world population suffers from it. For some people, sneezing fits can be triggered by hair combing, eyebrow tweezing, or even eating too much.

That's Wild!

If the DNA elements that make up a single human cell were written in <u>this size type</u>, the letter string would stretch . . .

a. almost 500 miles.
b. more than 10,000 miles.
c. just under 1,000 miles.
d. 20,000 miles.

Taxiing Work:

The part of the brain that's related to your sense of direction is called the posterior hippocampus. Researchers at University College in London, England, scanned the brains of 50 male cabdrivers and 50 males who did not drive cabs. The posterior hippocampus in cabbies was bigger than that in non-cabdrivers, and bigger still in cabdrivers who had been at their job the longest. If storing a complex map of streets in your head and figuring out the best way to get from place to place can make your brain grow, maybe other kinds of mental exercise can, too!

Sniffing Things Out:

Scientists at Stanford University have discovered that nostrils are not equally good at identifying different scents. For example, a more open nostril is better at smelling pepper while a more closed nostril is better at smelling licorice. Nostrils take turns swelling, so sometimes the left nostril is better at smelling something, and other times, the right one is. Try it yourself. Cover up one nostril at a time and compare their sniffing power.

Laugh Track:

To find out which part of the human brain reacts to humor, scientists at London's Institute of Neurology hooked up 14 people to a brain-imaging scanner and told them funny jokes. As the scientists monitored

the computer, they saw that the prefrontal cortex, an area of the brain right behind the forehead, lit up every time a joke was told. The funnier the joke, the brighter this area got. So it looks like people have a funny "bone" after all—it's just in the head, not in the elbow.

How Sweet It Is!

Researchers at Harvard University have located the gene that makes it possible for a mouse's taste buds to identify sweets. Not only that, but they have determined that differences in that gene dictate whether a mouse will prefer plain or sweetened water. If these same differences apply to human genes, it may go a long way to explaining why some people have a sweet tooth and others don't!

That's Wild!

Researchers Chittaranjan Andrade and B. S. Srihari have published an article in the *Journal of Clinical Psychiatry* on *rhinotillexomania,* the scientific name for . . .

a. bed-wetting.
b. hair-pulling.
c. pimple-popping.
d. nose-picking.

No Bones About It: Your funny bone isn't really a bone but the ulnar nerve, which runs from your neck through your armpit and down your arm to your hand and little finger. Where it crosses the elbow, the nerve is close to the surface. So when you bang your elbow just right, the nerve gets squeezed. This gives you a funny feeling—an intense tingling sensation shooting down your arm into your little finger. Incidentally, the name of the long bone in your upper arm is called the humerus. No pun intended.

A Bellyful: A survey on bellybutton lint, conducted by ABC Science Online, has revealed that the older you get, the more bellybutton lint you will accumulate. People with extremely hairy bellies and those with no hair at all had less lint than those with moderate hair. Males had more lint than females, and "innies" had more lint than "outies." Of the 4,799 people who participated, 66 percent had bellybutton lint.

Thumbs-Up:

According to a recent study, using high-tech gadgets, such as cell phones and handheld video games, has caused a physical mutation in today's youth.

Research conducted in nine cities around the world shows that the thumbs of people under age 25 have replaced the index finger as the most useful digit.

Weighty Results:

Research conducted in Britain suggests that you can get into shape just by thinking about it! Eighteen subjects were divided into three groups. The first group exercised their pinky fingers twice a week. The second group just thought about exercising, and the third group did nothing. The first group increased pinky strength by 33 percent, and the third group remained the same. However, pinkies in the second group got 16 percent stronger! Why? Increased brain activity sent faster signals to the muscles, improving performance.

That's Wild!

If all the nerves in a human adult's body were laid out end to end, their length would measure . . .

a. 47 feet.
b. 47 yards.
c. 47 inches.
d. 47 miles.

Magnet Man: Metal sticks to Liew Thow Lin's skin. With nuts, bolts, and tools dangling from his bare chest, Lin looks a lot like a walking hardware store. His ability stems from a medical condition that has nothing to do with magnets, but rather with a skin condition that results in a suction effect. Apparently the condition is genetic—Lin's three sons and two grandchildren all have the same ability.

Eye Strain: Avelino Perez got his kicks by popping his eyes right out of their sockets.

Alarming Condition: Victor Herbert of New York City sets off metal security detectors due to a condition called hemochromatosis, which caused 30 grams of iron—equal to a handful of nails—to build up inside his body.

That's Wild!

Synesthesia is a brain disorder that makes . . .

a. people's skin turn blue.
b. people sleep 20 hours a day.
c. everything taste like bubble gum.
d. people see newsprint in color and taste flavors as shapes.

Bulls-Eye!

Shirley Santos of New Bedford, Massachusetts, has an arrowhead-shaped birthmark in the iris of her right eye, and her twin brother has an identical marking in his left eye.

Don't Forget to Floss! Too small to see without a microscope but not too small to smell, bacteria are a major source of bad breath. And you have about a billion of them on each tooth! Why so many? Because your mouth is warm and damp—and because of the smorgasbord of food trapped between your teeth. Even after brushing, each tooth is still host to 100,000 of these tiny creatures!

The Good Guys: Sure, bacteria are responsible for causing diseases like strep throat and Lyme disease, not to mention bad breath and stinky feet. But bacteria also do good things, like turning milk into yogurt. Bacteria are used to make streptomycin, an antibiotic. And without bacteria in your gut, you wouldn't be able to digest your food.

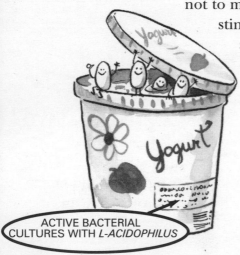

ACTIVE BACTERIAL CULTURES WITH *L-ACIDOPHILUS*

Blue Bloods: The United States government is limiting the amount of horseshoe crabs that can be used for bait. Why? Because there's something in these odd-looking creatures' blue-colored blood that scientists use to test for bacteria in medicines. Each year, about 300,000 crabs are bled and then placed back into their natural habitat. The process is quick and painless, and the crabs are no worse for wear.

Buggin' Out: Did you know that as you read this, 8,000 bacteria are camping out on each square inch of your legs? If that's not enough to make your skin crawl, you may be interested to know that at any given time nearly two million bacteria call your face home!

That's Wild!

There are more microbes (tiny organisms that can only be seen with a microscope) on a person's hand than there are . . .

a. shells in the ocean.
b. insects in the world.
c. people on Earth.
d. stars in the universe.

Deadly Saliva: Found only on a few islands in
Indonesia, Komodo dragons are fierce predators.
Even if an attack from one of these giant lizards
doesn't instantly kill an animal, the victim will still be
dead within 24 hours. That's because of all the bacteria
in the Komodo dragon's saliva. Yet Komodo dragons are
immune to one another's bites. Why? That's what
researcher Terry Fredieking hopes to find out.

Maggot Medicine: Maggots, nature's tiniest
microsurgeons, are used as a last resort when
conventional medical treatments have failed and
amputation is the only option. Bred in a special lab,
the maggots clean wounds by eating dead tissue and
harmful bacteria. There's only one catch—they have to
be removed within 72 hours or they'll turn into flies.

Thick-Skinned:

In 1992, American biochemists developed a painkiller from the skin of the tiny phantasmal poison frog found in Ecuador. The painkiller is 200 times stronger than morphine.

Ribbit-ing Discovery:

Dr. Michael A. Zasloff discovered that magainin, a substance found in the skin of African clawed frogs, helps fight infections that set in after a patient has had surgery.

Prey for a Cure:

The venom used by scorpions to paralyze their prey will soon be tested as a cure for patients with brain tumors. The venom affects the electrical activity of cancer cells and seems to stop the tumors from growing.

hello!

Downright Ear-y: British surgeons grafted Patrick Neary's severed right ear onto his thigh in an effort to regenerate the ear before reattaching it to his head.

Way to Go!
In 1990, scientists at Cambridge University in England were working on a cure for baldness and successfully grew hair in a test tube.

That's Wild!

No wonder it's so easy to catch a cold. The drops of moisture from a sneeze have been known to travel as fast as . . .

a. 150 feet per second.
b. a speeding bullet.
c. a running cheetah.
d. 90 miles per hour.

To find some truly bizarre facts, you need look no farther than your own body. Three of these amazing statements about the human body are the real deal. Can you spot the one impostor?

a. At birth, the human body has about 300 bones. But by the time we reach adulthood, many of our bones have fused together, leaving us with only about 206.

Believe It!   **Not!**

b. A human heart beats approximately 100,000 times a day.

Believe It!   **Not!**

c. The strongest muscle in the human body is in the big toe.

Believe It!   **Not!**

d. The acid in your stomach, which breaks down food, is strong enough to dissolve certain metals.

Believe It!   **Not!**

BONUS GAME
What's the Wonder?

Small but powerful, these wonders have roots and a hard outer layer. In fact, they are the toughest part of the human body! Just what are these wonders?

— — — — —

The world is full of natural wonders that are more incredible than even the most creative science-fiction writer could imagine!

Look Out Below!

Penny Boston and Diana Northup are two scientists who study caves, spending their days in a world of green slime and black ooze that smells a lot like rotting eggs. Why do they do it? One reason is to look for life-forms  that don't need sunlight to live. Some scientists think that life on Earth existed underground before it moved to the surface. If that's so, there may be life on Mars after all. It may just take a while to get down to it!

That's Wild!

A pipe organ in the Luray Caverns in Virginia was built using . . .

a. the caverns' stalactites.
b. copper pipes.
c. the caverns' stalagmites.
d. the ivory of ancient mammoths that died there.

Road-Kill Bouquet: Titan arum, also called the corpse flower, is found in the jungles of Indonesia. When they bloom, they smell like rotting flesh. The fact that they reek is why they survive. A flowering arum sends up an eight-foot-tall spear that, when heated by the sun, gives off a smell that can travel for miles. This is important because the plants grow few and far between. Their stench attracts insects, which then carry pollen from one plant to another.

The Exterminator: When a hungry insect bites into a passion vine, a tiny built-in cyanide "bomb" is released, killing the bug. Pretty neat, except there's one bug it doesn't work on. The caterpillar of the *Heliconius sara* butterfly is able to neutralize the poison and go right on eating. Good thing, since the passion vine is the only kind of plant it eats!

Fruit Alert: Durian is a large, spiny, tropical fruit with a really bad odor. So bad that a box of it stored in the baggage hold of a plane in Brisbane, Australia, caused a four-hour delay. Officials, fearing the worst, issued a full-scale hazardous chemical alert as fire crews evacuated and sealed off the plane. A big favorite of many people in Southeast Asia, durian has been banned from Singapore's subways and many of its restaurants due to its foul, overpowering smell.

No Exit: The bladderwort, an aquatic plant that floats in ponds, has trapdoors in its leaves through which tiny water organisms enter but can never leave. Gases released from the dead bodies of the organisms help keep the plant afloat.

That's Wild!

Spanish moss, which hangs in gray, gauzy clumps from trees in the southern part of the United States, is not really moss but a . . .

a. member of the pineapple family.
b. member of the cactus family.
c. type of fungus.
d. type of aromatic herb.

It's a Mirage! The sundew plant has hairs on its leaves, which glisten in the sun like drops of dew. The fake moisture lures thirsty insects—which the plants then smother and devour.

Take That! When attacked by caterpillars, willow trees change the chemical content of their leaves, lowering their nutritional value and making them less digestible.

Fee, Fie, Foe, Fum: Seaweed can grow two feet in one day—by far the fastest growth rate for any plant on Earth. Seaweed harvesters cut off only the tops of the plants. Then they extract a chemical called algin, which is used in more than 300 products, from salad dressing to textiles.

That's Wild!

To supply enough paper for a week's worth of newspapers in the United States, you would have to cut down . . .

a. 500,000 trees.
b. 1,000 trees.
c. 500 trees.
d. 50,000 trees.

Tree-mendous!

In Santa Maria del Tule, Mexico, there is a 2,000-year-old cypress tree that stands 138 feet tall, weighs about 700 tons, and measures 190 feet around its base—a circumference roughly equal to 19 cars placed end to end in a circle!

Em-barking: The canoe palm, which grows in the Amazon region of South America, has a huge bulge in its trunk. Slice it in half, and you will have a very functional canoe.

Drive-Through Tree Trunk:

In 1881, the 234-foot-tall Wawona Tree in Yosemite National Park, California, became the first living giant sequoia tree to have a tunnel cut through its trunk. The tunnel was 26 feet long, the diameter of the tree. After surviving for more than 2,000 years, the Wawona fell in 1969.

Mutant Ninja Frogs:

In 1995, a group of middle-school students in Le Sueur, Minnesota, made an alarming discovery. In the wetlands near their school, they found hundreds of deformed frogs—some with too many legs, some with too few legs, and some with other missing body parts. The reason for the concern? Frogs are more sensitive to the environment than other animals because they absorb air and water through their skin. Scientists are trying to find out what's going on before we start seeing six-legged humans as well!

That's Wild!

Don Juan Pond in Wright Valley, Antarctica, has such a high salt content that . . .

a. indigenous fish have developed a protective covering over their eyes.
b. Antarctica has become the biggest exporter of salt.
c. swimmers emerge with a terrible rash, called salt burn.
d. it never freezes, even at temperatures of minus 63°F.

Really Slick!

Have you ever wondered how it's possible to clean up after an oil spill from a huge oil tanker at sea? Bacteria are the answer. They suck up the oil and return it to the water in the form of harmless substances.

Good Pickin's: In 1992, scientists at Michigan State University altered the genes of a mouse-ear cress, a member of the mustard plant family, so that it produced biodegradable plastic. Now if they could just make money grow on trees!

Old Salt: Drs. Russell Vreeland and William Rosenzweig of West Chester University in Pennsylvania discovered bacteria, called *Bacillus permians,* that have been dormant inside a salt crystal for 250 million years!

How Big?

Fossil hunter and paleontologist Arturo Vildozola discovered dozens of giant oyster fossils in the Peruvian Andes. Some were up to six feet wide and would have produced football-size pearls!

That's Wild!

If you compressed Earth's history into a 24-hour day, dinosaurs would appear around 10:00 P.M. and humans would arrive just seconds before midnight. But bacteria would have made their entrance at . . .

a. noon.
b. 5:00 A.M.
c. 3:00 P.M.
d. 6:00 P.M.

Petrified Puke: One day, 160 million years ago, an ichthyosaur threw up. How do we know? Because paleontologists found 160 million–year-old fossilized vomit in an English quarry in 2002. The vomit contained

the remains of shellfish. Vomiting was probably how the ancient marine reptile expelled the shells that otherwise might have damaged its digestive system.

Leaves Clues: Scientist Jennifer McElwain of the Field Museum in Chicago, Illinois, is studying 200 million–year-old plant fossils in order to learn more about global warming. Many scientists believe that the mass extinction of prehistoric life at that time was caused by too much carbon dioxide in the air. By studying fossilized leaves, McElwain hopes to understand what might happen to today's plant and animal life should the levels of carbon dioxide double in the next 100 years, as many scientists are predicting.

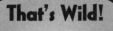

The Big Sink: New York City was looking for a way to get rid of its old, retired subway cars. The state of Delaware was looking for large objects to serve as artificial reefs. The perfect solution to both problems was arrived at in 2002 when 400 subway cars, minus motors, wheels, windows, and seats, were sunk off the coast of Delaware. Scientists hope that blue mussels will attach themselves to the cars' hard surfaces. If they do, it won't be long before the waters are teeming with black sea bass and gray triggerfish, which live on a diet of blue mussels.

Surf's Up! Scientists in Australia have identified a giant wave circling Antarctica, which is as large as the Australian continent and almost a mile deep!

That's Wild!

You can actually squeeze 600 billion trillion atoms into . . .

a. an eight-ounce thermos.
b. a jar of baby food.
c. a thimble.
d. a teapot.

Bubble Trouble:

What happens to all those ships that mysteriously disappear when they enter the Bermuda Triangle? The answer just might be bubbles. When Naval scientist Bruce Denardo and his colleagues forced air bubbles underneath some balls in a beaker of water, the balls sank. Apparently, the airy water was not heavy enough to support the balls. Beneath the oceans, there are large pockets of methane hydrate, a combination of swamp gas and water. A change in temperature or pressure can cause the gas to come bubbling up, possibly creating enough bubbles to sink a ship!

Wide, Wide World:

Since 1998, Earth's circumference has increased by about an eighth of an inch. Scientists at Maryland's NASA Goddard Space Flight Center suspect that the change has been caused by shifting ocean currents that are sending seawater toward the equator.

That's a Lotta Cabbage!

In Alaska, John and Mary Evans specialize in growing giant vegetables. Their daughter, Lauren, is following in their footsteps with the 76-pound cabbage that she grew in 1998. Anyone for coleslaw?

The Great Pumpkin: On October 12, 1998, the Half Moon Bay Art and Pumpkin Festival in California opened with the 25th Annual Great Pumpkin Weigh-off. The winner was the 974-pound monster being pushed onto the scales at right.

Chocolate Toothpaste?

After three months of drinking water that was fortified with cocoa bean husks, laboratory rats developed fewer cavities. Researchers at Japan's Osaka University have determined that the outer shells of cocoa beans contain antibacterial agents that could be added to toothpaste. *Yum!*

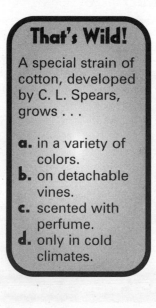

That's Wild!

A special strain of cotton, developed by C. L. Spears, grows . . .

a. in a variety of colors.
b. on detachable vines.
c. scented with perfume.
d. only in cold climates.

Taters for Tot: Soon kids may be able to eat french fries instead of getting shots! Scientists are altering the genes of potatoes to give them built-in vaccines. At Loma Linda Medical School in California, a potato with a built-in vaccine for cholera—a disease that kills three million children a year worldwide—has been successfully tested on mice. This could greatly benefit children who live in poor countries and can't afford expensive vaccines.

Just Listed! The Island of Surtsey rose from the sea off Iceland after a volcanic explosion in 1967. Two years later, it measured two and a half square miles and had plants growing on it.

The Refrigerator Fish: In 1989, scientists in Boulder, Colorado, discovered that blood from a fish found in Antarctica contains chemicals that can keep ice cream and other frozen foods from thawing!

That's Wild!

In 1966, more than 1,600 people died in Cameroon, West Africa, when Lake Nyos . . .

a. overflowed its banks.
b. spewed lava from an underground volcano.
c. became polluted from the illegal dumping of toxic waste.
d. released a cloud of deadly carbon dioxide.

Brain Buster

Earthquakes, volcanoes, tidal waves—Earth has all kinds of natural wonders! So it's not hard to believe that three of the following statements are actually true. Can you spot the one that's out of this world?

a. Mount Everest, the tallest mountain in the world, grows two inches taller every year!

Believe It!   **Not!**

b. There are more than 1,500 active volcanoes on Earth—but luckily, most of them are buried beneath the sea.

Believe It!   **Not!**

c. Alaska has more earthquakes in a year than all 49 of the other states combined.

Believe It!   **Not!**

d. The tallest tree on Earth stands a whopping 50 feet tall and is called the Bedwood Tree, named after its hometown in Bedford, Minnesota.

Believe It!   **Not!**

BONUS GAME
What's the Wonder?

This wonder, which covers 75 percent of Earth's surface, comes in all shapes and sizes. It can be wide or narrow, shallow or deep. Though it might seem to be many different colors, it is colorless in its natural state. What's the wonder?

— — — — —

Each venture into space delivers new clues to the secrets of the universe—as well as technological advances that improve the quality of life on Earth.

Seeing Stars: Since its launching in 1993, the Hubble telescope has become our eye on the universe. It has recorded evidence of energy-eating black holes, taken photos of a comet crashing into Jupiter, and even captured images of the birth and death of stars!

That's Wild!

When large stars die, first they explode, then they collapse into a small, dense star. If one of these baseball-size stars could be brought to Earth, it would weigh more than . . .

a. a space shuttle.
b. an elephant.
c. a freight train.
d. the Empire State Building.

Martian Garden: In 2001, plants were grown in Martian soil for the first time by scientist Michael Mautner of Lincoln University in New Zealand. How did he do it? By grinding up pieces of two meteorites. Mautner was

able to confirm that his meteorites were from Mars by comparing the chemical composition of gas bubbles trapped inside them with gas that was analyzed in the 1970s by NASA's first and second *Viking* spacecraft. The tiny asparagus and potatoes grown in the Martian soil are evidence that it might be possible for future colonies on Mars to grow their own food there.

Whew! On March 23, 1989, an asteroid larger than an aircraft carrier, traveling at a speed of about 46,000 miles per hour, missed Earth by only six hours—or about 43,000 miles. Considering it's believed that a huge asteroid wiped out the dinosaurs, it's a good thing this one missed us!

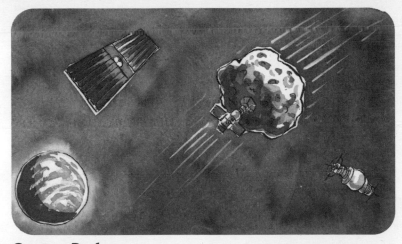

Getting Pushy: Though the chances of Earth being slammed by an asteroid are extremely slim, a group of astronauts and scientists, headed by *Apollo 9* astronaut Russell Schweickart, would like to be prepared if an asteroid heads our way anytime soon. Their idea calls for a spacecraft to meet up with the asteroid, stop it from spinning, and push it out of harm's way!

Rock On: It's only once in a blue moon that you might be lucky enough to come across a meteorite from Mars or the moon. Only about 24 moon rocks and 16 Martian meteorites had ever been found. But in 2001, two rare rocks from space turned up in the Sahara desert in northern Africa—a moon rock weighing a little more than two pounds and a meteorite from Mars weighing barely an ounce.

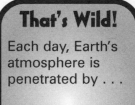

That's Wild!

Each day, Earth's atmosphere is penetrated by . . .

a. five comets.
b. 75,000,000 meteors.
c. ten asteroids.
d. 10,000 chunks of space ice.

A Piece of the Rock: These days, meteorites are selling for thousands of dollars an ounce—way too expensive for museums to buy. So in order to update their collections, museums have been forced to trade old specimens for new ones. The American Museum of Natural History's planetarium recently sold a piece of the Willamette Meteorite, the 15.5-ton centerpiece of their collection. In return, they received a small piece of a meteorite from Mars. The buyer of the chunk of the Willamette Meteorite sliced off a 4.5-pound piece, which he auctioned off for $11,000!

Polyps in Space:

NASA scientists want to learn how zero gravity affects humans, so they're studying the development of jellyfish polyps in space. Why jellyfish? Because they have special gravity receptors with calcium crystals that help them  swim and orient themselves. Humans have similar crystals in the inner ears that help maintain balance. So studying baby jellyfish growing can help us learn how human babies might grow in a spaceship!

Heaven Scent:

In November 1998, a rose plant was placed aboard NASA's space shuttle *Discovery* Flight STS-95 in an experiment to find out what would happen to an essential oil under zero-gravity conditions. Scientists thought the fragrance would change, but the results were even more dramatic than they expected. The rose produced an entirely new scent that was out of this world. Named the "space rose" scent, it was used by Shiseido Cosmetics in 2000 to produce a perfume called Zen.

Heart to Heart:

There was an extra passenger on the historical 1998 *Discovery* mission— a working artificial heart used to study the effects of space on astronauts, whose hearts can shrink by about 15 percent during flight.

That's Wild!

Invented by the Langley Research Center, riblits—tiny grooves that are used on aircraft to reduce friction— have been adapted for use . . .

a. in swimsuits for athletes.
b. as a nonskid surface around swimming pools.
c. on the soles of bedroom slippers.
d. in baby clothes and shoes.

Arachno-philia:

Imagine sending a group of tiny robots equipped with cameras to another planet where they could spread out, talk to one another, and send information back

to scientists on Earth. Imagine that they have antennas to detect obstacles and that they have legs so they can climb around craters and over jagged rocks. The seven-inch-tall Spider-bot, developed for NASA by engineer Robert Hogg, can do all these things and more.

Totally Spacey: Zero

gravity makes actions that are impossible on Earth a breeze in space. Midair somersaults and lifting heavy equipment are a snap. On the other hand, things we take for granted on Earth are much more of a challenge. Drinking and eating require special consideration. When drinks escape from their containers, they float around the spacecraft as giant bubbles!

High-Tech.

Robo-roach: In an experiment at the University of Tokyo, scientists attached electronic mini backpacks to cockroaches and replaced their antennae with electrodes. This allowed the scientists to direct the bugs' movements by remote control.

Tooth Implant: Two British researchers have created a model for a high-tech receiver that can be embedded in your molar. A caller's voice would be turned into vibrations that travel through your skull to your inner ear—where only you can hear them.

Getting the Latest News: A company called E Ink Corporation predicts that in a few years, RadioPaper, a thin, flexible surface coated with electronic ink plus a backplate equipped with transistors, will allow readers to update their newspapers on demand.

Plant-zilla!

The Better to Eat You! Only meat will satisfy the hunger of some unusual plants that grow in the rain forests of Southeast Asia. Frogs, birds, and rats can be digested by the *Nepenthes* plant (right).

Pee-ew! The titan arum (left) of Indonesia is one flower you don't want to stop and smell. Also known as the corpse flower, its scent has been compared to rotting roadkill.

The Better to Sting You! New Zealand's tree nettle (right) grows more than nine feet tall. Toxins coat the fine hairs that line its branches. Dogs, horses, and at least one human have died from touching this dangerous plant.

Mean and Green: Just two millionths of an ounce of poison from the seeds (circle) of the castor bean plant (right) can kill a person weighing 158 pounds. The poison, called *ricin*, is 12,000 times more powerful than the venom of a rattlesnake!

Fruit Most Foul! In Southeast Asia, some people call durian the "king of fruit." But that hasn't stopped the subways and restaurants of Indonesia from banning it because of its extremely foul smell!

Mad Medicine

Blood Banks: Scientists are using the blood of horseshoe crabs to test medicine for bacteria. Each year, they bleed about 300,000 crabs, then return them to their natural habitat.

Long-distance Surgery: In 2001, a surgeon working in New York removed the gall bladder of a woman in a hospital in France. With the aid of a video camera and a high-speed fiber-optic line, the surgeon manipulated the arm of a surgical robot to perform the operation.

Feeling Wired: Instead of drilling a hole in the skull, Dr. Demetrius Lopes (right) used a thin magnet-tipped wire to perform brain surgery on Paul Kelsey. Lopes guided the wire through tiny blood vessels in the brain with the help of a magnet suspended above Kelsey's head.

What a Pill! Sometimes doctors have to snake a tube down a patient's throat to detect a problem. Now there's a better way—a video camera that fits inside a pill. Once the pill is swallowed, a receiver picks up images that the doctor can see on a computer.

Komodo Cure: The bacteria in a Komodo dragon's saliva can kill prey in 24 hours, but will not affect another Komodo dragon. No one knows why, but researcher Terry Fredieking thinks solving this mystery may hold a key to strengthening the human immune system.

Really

Far Out: In the 1600s, Galileo was the first person to look at the stars with a telescope. But what he saw was nothing like what we can see today. Powerful technology like the Hubble Space Telescope (above), lets us see stars that are billions of light-years away. And because it takes their light so long to reach us, we're seeing the stars not as they look now, but as they looked billions of years in the past.

Making an Impact: In 1994, the Hubble Space Telescope photographed fragments of the comet Shoemaker-Levy-9 crashing into the planet Jupiter.

Spacey

A Star Is Born: Nebulas are huge masses of gas where new stars are born. When a part of a nebula gets dense enough, gravity causes it to shrink. As the clump gets smaller, it gets hot enough to set off nuclear reactions and become a new star.

Going Out with a Bang! After billions of years, stars start to burn out. As they cool, they expand. The biggest ones become red supergiants. These supergiants go out in a spectacular explosion called a supernova. The image above shows gases left by a supernova that occurred about 1,600 years ago.

Looking into the Past: In 2003, data from the WMAP satellite was used to compile a map of the universe as it looked just 380,000 years after the Big Bang created it 13.7 billion years ago.

Oddly Experimental

Static Cling: Ever wonder why geckos are able to walk upside down? Scientists have discovered it's because there are millions of tiny hairs on the geckos' feet. Tiny electrical charges in the hairs and on the walking surface attract one another, allowing the lizards to cling to almost anything.

Mite-y Dedication: Dr. Robert A. Lopez transplanted ear mites from cats' ears to his own! What did he find out? The host can feel and hear the mites as they scurry around the ear canal.

Milking Music: Researchers at England's University of Leicester piped music into a dairy barn holding 1,000 cows. What was the animals' favorite song? Simon and Garfunkel's "Bridge Over Troubled Water." Milk production increased by three percent.

Potties in Space: One thing robots don't have to deal with in space is going to the bathroom. For humans, suction toilets are the way to go. They work like vacuum cleaners. A flow of air sucks the waste into a container. And, Believe It or Not!, on the *Mir* space station, fluid waste is recycled into drinking water!

Up Against It! Instead of hitting the sack, some astronauts prefer to float freely in zero gravity. Others zip themselves into sleeping bags that are attached to the wall. Since there is no up or down in space, it doesn't really matter where you rest your head.

That's Wild!

Scientists at NASA have discovered that thousands of house-sized snowballs . . .

a. bombard Earth's atmosphere every day.
b. float freely in the atmosphere of Jupiter.
c. clog the volcanos on Venus.
d. form the rings of Saturn.

The Right Track:

Developed by NASA's Jet Propulsion Laboratory and LC Technologies, the Eyegaze System enables severely disabled people to communicate using only their eyes. Nothing is attached to the user's head or body. A video camera is focused on the user's eye to track its movement. So to "press" a key on the screen, all the user has to do is look at that key for a specific amount of time, and the computer will follow the command!

Clean Start:

Driving cars that run on hydrogen-powered fuel cells could make air pollution a thing of the past. The cells release water vapor instead of greenhouse gases like fossil fuels do, and were first used in the space program in the 1960s. One problem facing the auto industry is how to store the hydrogen at the necessary minus 418°F and still be able to make the cars widely available. Honda is using a type of hydrogen that can be stored at normal temperatures in its 2003 FCX, the first hydrogen-powered car to meet United States standards for zero emissions.

Fin-tastic: The Dukane Corporation has designed NetMark 1000 to help protect harbor porpoises from being caught and killed in nets meant to catch bottom fish. The technology was originally developed in the late 1960s by NASA engineers at the Langley Research Center to help locate NASA cargo after watery touchdowns. NetMark 1000 gives off pinging signals that warn porpoises that a net is near.

That's Wild!

Advanced sensor technology to improve the mobility of robots in space has resulted in . . .

a. Park Smart, a device to help motorists find a parking spot in public garages.
b. Robo-Lift, a robot that can carry grocery bags from the car to the house.
c. Jiffy Belt, a seat belt that exercises stomach muscles.
d. Trash Bot, a walking trash can that takes out the garbage.

Medical Marvels: Here on Earth, the foam insulation that covers the space shuttle's outer fuel tank is being used to make prosthetics, such as artificial arms and legs. NASA technology that is used to measure the temperatures of stars is also being used in ear thermometers to measure a person's body temperature. And NASA-funded research resulted in precision-guided robotic arms that have been used in surgery— and hopefully will be used on future space repair missions, too.

Brain Buster

It's a bird! It's a plane! It's . . . a brain buster from outer space! Can you spot the one space invader in this list of far-out facts about our galaxy?

a. Mars may be the closest planet, but it would still take astronauts sixty years to reach it.
Believe It!   **Not!**

b. Everyone knows that Saturn has thousands of rings. But fewer people know that it also has 30 moons.
Believe It!   **Not!**

c. If the sun were the size of a grapefruit, then Earth would be the size of a pencil point.
Believe It!   **Not!**

d. A person who weighs 100 pounds on Earth would only weigh 38 pounds on Mercury.
Believe It!   **Not!**

BONUS GAME
What's the Wonder?

The smallest in our solar system by far, and quite a distance away from Earth, this planet actually rotates around the sun in the opposite direction as its eight siblings. It also overlaps its orbit with another planet— they trade off the honor of being the farthest planet from the sun. What's the wonder?

— — — — —

CHAPTER 5 High-Tech Wonders

Advances in technology have touched almost every aspect of our lives.

Off the Wall: American Technology's new speakers emit ultrasonic sound waves in a beam like that of a flashlight. You can only hear the sound if you step into the beam or if it is reflected off a surface. What difference does this make? Now marketers can target individual shoppers, lifeguards can call a message to a single swimmer without disturbing anyone else, and TV fans can get great sound by simply bouncing sound waves off the wall instead of installing speakers.

That's Wild!

In 1992, scientists in Great Britain invented a handheld sensor that tells people . . .

a. how long to stay in the sun.
b. when to come in out of the rain.
c. how to find the nearest ice-cream store.
d. when a pickpocket is about to steal their wallet.

63

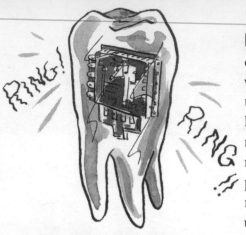

Phone Home: Tired of carrying a cell phone wherever you go? In the future, you may not have to. Instead of a mobile phone, you just might have a molar phone. Two British researchers have come up with a model for a "phone tooth." This high-tech receiver can be embedded in one of your own molars. Then, whenever someone calls you, his or her voice will be turned into vibrations that travel from the tooth through your skull to your inner ear, so only you can hear what's being said. The catch? You can only listen—you can't talk back!

Robo-roach: Insects can do many things that people can't—like crawl through earthquake rubble or slip through tight places on top secret spying missions. So scientists at the University of Tokyo created the perfect cyborg (a combination of computer hardware and living creature) to fill the bill. In this case, they replaced cockroaches' antennae with electrodes and attached electronic mini backpacks to them. Then, using a remote control, they sent signals that made the bugs move left, right, or straight ahead.

Back at You! An inventor in Great Britain has patented an unusual invention he calls the "anti-abuser." The device records an insult and then does one of a number of things, depending on how it's set. One option is to have the insult thrown back at the person who called it out. Another is to set off a piercing wail or screech. Now if a bully comes up and tries to grab your backpack, all you have to do is turn on your anti-abuser!

Remote, Remote Control: In 2001, the brain signals from a monkey hooked up to a computer in a North Carolina laboratory were sent via the Internet to control the movement of a robotic arm at a university 600 miles away. Believe It or Not!

That's Wild!

Belle, a computer developed by researchers at Bell Laboratories, was designed to . . .

a. analyze medical data.
b. teach sign language.
c. play chess.
d. keep track of the weather.

Sparkling Tribute:

When 80-year-old Edna MacArthur of Alberta, Canada, died, her family wanted something besides photos to remember her by. So they turned Grandma into a

diamond! A Canadian funeral company is the first to offer this service, which involves compressing a body into a three-gram sample. It is then flown to an Italian company that uses intense heat to convert the sample into carbon. It can then be crafted into a synthetic diamond. MacArthur's granddaughter says the family plans to have the stone set in a gold ring.

Feeling Chipper:

Computer whiz Derek Jacobs is a big fan of technology. At age 14, he convinced his family to be the first to have a rice-sized device called a VeriChip implanted in their arms. In an emergency, doctors can simply scan the chip to learn a patient's medical history, including such lifesaving information as whether they are allergic to any medicines.

What's the Score? Imagine checking the sports page to see how your favorite basketball team is doing and the score changes right before your eyes! A scene from a Harry Potter movie? Not quite. Actually, a company called E Ink predicts that within the next five to ten years, newspapers will continually update themselves as events unfold in real time. RadioPaper, invented by Barrett Comiskey and his colleagues at Massachusetts Institute of Technology, will make this dream a reality. A flexible surface coated with electronic ink that can be altered through digital technology, RadioPaper just might make newspapers as we know them a thing of the past!

That's Wild!

Scientists at the Almaden Research Laboratory in San Jose, California, have developed transmitters and receivers that transfer electronic messages through . . .

a. sunglasses.
b. the soles of shoes.
c. hats.
d. handshakes.

Silk from Milk: Stronger than steel and more flexible than a rubber band, spider silk is one fabulous fiber. With enough of it, you could make super ropes and indestructible fabrics. The catch? Unlike silkworms that get along fine on silk farms, spiders do nothing but fight when they're together. That's why researchers at Nexia Biotechnologies in Montreal, Canada, have come up with a way to place spider genes in the DNA of goats! The enhanced goats' milk contains spider silk proteins. Factories separate the proteins from the milk and weave it into silk. What's next? Spider milk?

That's Wild!

Using an electron-scanning microscope, the entire contents of the *Encyclopedia Britannica* can be written on . . .

a. a grain of rice.
b. one side of a dime.
c. one side of a quarter.
d. the head of a pin.

Eyewitness: Researchers in Minnesota have come up with a new kind of lie detector—a camera that records heat patterns as white areas on the skin. When a person tells a lie, the blood rushes to his or her face, increasing the temperature in that area. So when a test subject lied

in front of the camera, a white ring appeared around the eyes, immediately giving away the liar!

Look, Ma, No Drill: New ways to get to the brain are leading to a kinder, gentler form of brain surgery. In 2003, Dr. Demetrius Lopes snaked a thin wire with a tiny magnet on the end through Paul Kelsey's body to his

brain. A helmet-shaped magnet hanging over Kelsey's head helped the doctor guide the wire through the brain to the area where a swollen blood vessel needed attention. A squirt of glue sealed off the artery, and the surgery was complete.

Dressing Smart: Scientists at the Institute of Electronics at Tampere University in Finland have developed clothing embedded with computers that can measure vital signs and send out distress signals if the wearer becomes lost.

Smile! Some tests require doctors to run a tube down a patient's throat to see what's causing problems in a patient's intestines. Not a pleasant experience! Now some patients are in for a break. Doctors in Israel and England are using a video camera so tiny that it fits inside a pill. The patient, wearing a receiver about the size of a deck of cards, swallows the pill. The camera sends images to the receiver, which the doctor can see on a computer.

Toilet Training:

A high-tech toilet seat developed in Japan is attached to sensors that check the weight of users, measure the fat and sugar content of their wastes, and then transmit the results directly to doctors.

No Pain, Big Gain:

Mark Prausnitz and Mark Allen of the Georgia Institute of Technology have developed microneedles— needles that are so small, they only puncture the outer layer of skin. This is very good news. Why? This part of the skin has no nerves, so the punctures are painless!

That's Wild!

Scientists at a biotechnology company in East Germany, have patented fungi that . . .

a. can digest the cellulose base of plastic car bodies that have been scrapped.

b. are used in shampoo to get rid of head lice.

c. are used in landfills to dissolve disposable diapers.

d. are used in insecticide to kill mosquitoes on contact.

Cleaning Up: How would you like to have a house that cleaned itself? Frances Gabe thought housework was a boring, thankless job, so she decided to completely redesign her house. Now she can just push a button and sprays of soapy water clean an entire room and its waterproof furniture. Next a rinse, then a blow dry to get any water that didn't run down the drain in the sloping floors. Special cupboards wash, dry and store the dishes, and closets do the same for clothes. Altogether Gabe has patented more than 65 work-saving devices.

That's Wild!

Scientists at the Tongji University in Shanghai, China, have developed a paint that . . .

a. never fades.
b. cools in summer, warms in winter, and changes color with the seasons.
c. repels snow.
d. contains bug repellent.

Technology has brought us all kinds of crucial creations. And it's also given us some incredibly *insignificant* inventions! Four silly innovations are listed here. But can you spot the one that even the most imaginative inventor has not yet created?

a. An earring catcher that sits on your shoulder. Never lose an earring again!

> **Believe It!**   **Not!**

b. Self-tying shoelaces. You say "tie" and your laces will obey!

> **Believe It!**   **Not!**

c. A toilet light that reminds you if you've left the seat up.

> **Believe It!**   **Not!**

d. Dust mops that attach to cat's paws. Let your kitten clean the floors!

> **Believe It!**   **Not!**

BONUS GAME
What's the Wonder?

In 1873, a 15-year-old boy named Chester Greenwood was testing a new pair of ice skates when his ears got very cold. He wrapped his head in a scarf, but the scarf was too big and too itchy. To keep his ears warm and still be able to skate, Greenwood needed something smaller that he didn't have to keep adjusting. So, with a little sewing help from his grandmother, Greenwood invented this wonderful winter garb. What is this wearable wonder?

__ __ __ __ __ __ __ __

POP QUIZ

Just can't get enough shocking science facts? Great! Because here is one more chance to prove you've got an eye for the unbelievable. The following quiz is a review of all the weird and wacky wonders you've read about in this book. (And it's worth a ton of points for your brain busters score!) Pick up that pencil and show us how savvy you really are!

1. What song increased cows' milk productivity in a dairy barn in England?
a. "Home on the Range"
b. "Oops! I Did It Again"
c. "Bridge Over Troubled Water"
d. "The Farmer in the Dell"

2. Which of the following off-the-wall statements is true about geckos?
a. Geckos have an unusually potent scent that allows them to sense one another from up to ten miles away.
b. Geckos only eat lima beans.
c. Geckos can walk on ceilings.
d. Geckos can only be found in the wild in Madagascar.

3. Which one of these four extraordinary experiments has never happened?

a. PhD candidate Karyn Harmon did experiments with various breeds of chicken to try to discover which really came first—the chicken or the egg.

b. Physicist Robert Matthews tested Murphy's Law by having a thousand schoolchildren drop pieces of buttered toast to see which way they would land.

c. Scientists tested birds' ability to tell one artist from another by showing them paintings by different artists.

d. Two meteorologists did research to tell who will get wetter in the rain—someone running or walking.

4. Luak coffee beans, considered by some to make the best-tasting coffee in the world, are harvested after they have taken a trip through a luak's digestive system.

Believe It!   Not!

5. Scientists in England gave a memory test in which some subjects chewed gum, some did not, and others just pretended to chew gum. They found that . . .

a. the real gum chewers scored highest.

b. the non-chewers scored highest.

c. the pretend chewers scored the highest.

d. everyone scored the same.

6. Which of the following bizarre body facts is nothing but fiction?

a. Your "funny bone" is actually a nerve.

b. The older you get, the more bellybutton lint you get.

c. It is a proven fact that it's physically impossible to walk and chew gum at the same time.

d. Even after you brush, you have approximately 100,000 bacteria on each of your teeth.

7. Bacteria do NOT . . .
a. cause strep throat.
b. control the tides.
c. turn milk into yogurt.
d. cause stinky feet.

8. A Komodo dragon's bite is much worse than its bark. In fact, the only animal that is immune to the Komodo's bacteria-infested saliva is . . .
a. a pelican.
b. a human being.
c. a rattlesnake.
d. another Komodo dragon.

9. Durian is a large, spiny, tropical fruit that once caused a four-hour delay in an airport because . . .
a. it has a high metal content.
b. it really stinks.
c. it shakes and rattles uncontrollably.
d. its highly valuable seeds were stolen.

10. Seaweed can grow at a rate of 50 feet per day.
Believe It!   Not!

11. Chop down the one tree story below that isn't true.
a. The Wawona Tree in Yosemite National Park was the first living tree to have a tunnel cut through its trunk.
b. A cypress tree in Mexico has a circumference of 190 feet—which is the length of 19 cars placed end to end.
c. Willow trees can change the nutritional value of their leaves when they are under attack by most kinds of caterpillars.
d. Lumberjack Davie Grease chopped down an evergreen tree that was more than 20 stories tall.

12. When a rosebush was sent into space aboard the shuttle *Discovery*, what happened to it?
a. It gave off a foul smell.
b. Nothing. It stayed exactly the same.
c. It turned a different color.
d. It produced a brand new scent.

13. Astronauts have some pretty amazing adventures in space. But which of the following is artificial intelligence?
a. Weightlessness makes lifting heavy equipment a snap.
b. To keep up their strength while in space, astronauts must eat spinach at every meal.
c. Astronauts use suction toilets.
d. Astronauts often sleep in sleeping bags.

14. To replace the cell phone, researchers in Britain are working on a "nail phone." The receiver and speakers will be implanted in people's fingernails.
Believe It! **Not!**

15. Which of these unusual high-tech gizmos has not been invented?
a. An "anti-abuser" that throws insults back at people
b. A toilet seat that acts as a scale and a monitor of people's waste products
c. An animated photograph that speaks and moves
d. A lie detector camera

Answer Key

Chapter 1
Wacky Research

Page 5:   **b.** they swallow plastic pot scrubbers.

Page 6:   **c.** shock absorbers for cars.

Page 8:   **d.** disposable diapers.

Page 10:   **d.** Wasps

Page 13:   **a.** a teapot spout that won't drip.

Page 15:   **a.** can get seasick.

Page 16   **c.** 100 years old.

Brain Buster: d. is false.

Bonus Game: carbon dioxide

Chapter 2
Bizarre Body Matters

Page 19:   **d.** an oil tanker more than 46 times.

Page 21:   **b.** more than 10,000 miles.

Page 23:   **d.** nose-picking.

Page 25:   **d.** 47 miles.

Page 27:   **d.** people see newsprint in color and taste flavors as shapes.

Page 29:   **c.** people on Earth.

Page 31:   **c.** an entire ballpark.

Page 32:   **a.** 150 feet per second.

Brain Buster: c. is false.

Bonus Game: teeth

Chapter 3
What in the World?

Page 35: **a.** the caverns' stalactites.

Page 37: **a.** member of the pineapple family.

Page 38: **a.** 500,000 trees.

Page 40: **d.** it never freezes, even at temperatures of minus 63°F.

Page 42: **b.** 5:00 A.M.

Page 44: **c.** a thimble.

Page 47: **a.** in a variety of colors.

Page 48: **d.** released a cloud of deadly carbon dioxide.

Brain Buster: d. is false.

Bonus Game: water

Chapter 4
Out of This World

Page 51: **b.** an elephant.

Page 53: **b.** 75,000,000 meteors.

Page 55: **a.** in swimsuits for athletes.

Page 57: **a.** bombard Earth's atmosphere every day.

Page 59: **a.** Park Smart, a device to help motorists find a parking spot in public garages.

Page 60: **b.** Vomit Comet.

Brain Buster: a. is false.

Bonus Game: Pluto

Chapter 5
High-Tech Wonders

Page 63: **a.** how long to stay in the sun.

Page 65: **c.** play chess.

Page 67: **d.** handshakes.

Page 68: **d.** the head of a pin.

Page 71: **a.** can digest the cellulose base of plastic car bodies that have been scrapped.

Page 72: **b.** cools in summer, warms in winter, and changes color with the seasons.

Brain Buster: b. is false.

Bonus Game: earmuffs

Pop Quiz

1. **c.**
2. **c.**
3. **a.**
4. **Believe It!**
5. **a.**
6. **c.**
7. **b.**
8. **d.**
9. **b.**
10. **Not!**
11. **d.**
12. **d.**
13. **b.**
14. **Not!**
15. **c.**

What's Your Ripley's Rank?

Ripley's Scorecard

Time's up! You're through experimenting, so what's the conclusion? You've explored all kinds of oddball scientific notions in the brain-busting activities. Now it's time to tally up your answers and get your Ripley's rating. Are you **Still Experimenting**? Or are you already a **Mad Scientist**? Add up your scores to find out!

Here's the scoring breakdown. Give yourself:

★ **10 points** for every **That's Wild!** you answered correctly;

★ **20 points** for every fiction you spotted in the **Ripley's Brain Busters**;

★ **10 points** every time you solved a **What's the Wonder?**;

★ and **5 points** for every **Pop Quiz** question you got right.

Here's a tally sheet:

Number of **That's Wild!**
questions answered correctly: _____ x 10 = _____
Number of **Ripley's Brain Buster**
fictions spotted: _____ x 20 = _____
Number of **What's the Wonder?**
puzzles solved: _____ x 10 = _____
Number of **Pop Quiz** questions
answered correctly: _____ x 5 = _____

Total the right column for your final score: _____

0–100
Still Experimenting

You're not exactly running to throw on a lab coat and
fire up the Bunsen burner. Maybe your science teacher
gives you the creeps or you find yourself sleeping
through astronomy? Well—WAKE UP!—and notice all
the wacky and fun facts all around you. Even if science
isn't your fave, there are tons of other Ripley's subjects
for your experimenting pleasure. More of a history buff?
Try *Blasts from the Past*. Or check out *Creepy Stuff* to
uncover freaky facts that will scare you silly!

101–250
Scientific Methods

You're starting to get a knack for sorting out these
wacky Believe It or Not! facts. Now you just need to
brush up on some scientific know-how. Plant life, the
solar system, the wacky world of high-tech gadgets and
gizmos—there is so much out there to experiment with!
And the more you know, the odder and more bizarre it
will get. Believe It!

251–400
That's the Idea!

You must be on a mission to download everything you can about radical research and extraordinary experiments! You are in the know about all things science-related. Plus, you can tell the real deals from make-believe. You may not get every single brain buster right, but with a little more Ripley's practice, you will be breezing right by with your serious science savvy!

401–575
Mad Scientist!

Okay, time to come out of the laboratory and take a little break! You know everything there is to know about bizarre science. Even the frightening little details about plant specimens are like second nature to you! You are a Ripley's dynamo, it's true. But maybe it's time to expand your horizons—and perhaps try a little Shakespeare on for size?

Photo Credits

Ripley Entertainment Inc. and the editors of this book wish to thank the following photographers, agents, and other individuals for permission to use and reprint the following photographs in this book. Any photographs included in this book that are not acknowledged below are property of the Ripley Archives. Great effort has been made to obtain permission from the owners of all materials included in this book. Any errors that may have been made are unintentional and will gladly be corrected in future printings if notice is sent to Ripley Entertainment Inc., 5728 Major Boulevard, Orlando, Florida 32819.

Black & White Photos

3   Milky Way; 31 Scorpion/Ablestock

7   Under-Ease/Courtesy Under-Tec Corp./www.under-tec.com

8   Costumed Pilot in Ultralight/PR Newswire Photo Service

10 Hurricane/Courtesy NOAA

12 Landfill/© Digital Vision/PictureQuest

14 Wave/PhotoDisc Blue

16 Luak/© Mark Kostich/www.kostich.com

20 Zebrafish/Courtesy University of California San Francisco

22 London Cab/© Creatas/PictureQuest

25 Game Players/Digital Vision

29 Horseshoe Crabs/Jonathan Barth/Getty

37 Durian/© Isabelle Rosenbaum/PhotoAlto/PictureQuest

39 Wawona Tree/Courtesy of Jarl de Boer

41 Oil Spill/© D. Falconer/PhotoLink/Photodisc/PictureQuest

43 Jennifer McElwain/Milbert O. Brown/KRT

44 Redbird Subway Cars/© Daniel Choy Boyar

46 Giant Pumpkin/Terry Schmitt/UPI Photo Service

48 Surtsey/Yann Arthus-Bertrand/CORBIS

51 Hubble Telescope; 56 Spiderbot; 60 NASA Prosthetics/Courtesy of NASA

52 Asparagus Tissue/Courtesy Michael Mautner

54 Willamette Meteorite/Ben Fraser

58 Honda Fuel-Cell Car/© 2001 American Honda Motor Co., Inc., and Wieck Media Services, Inc.

64 Roboroach; 70 Video-camera Pill/Reuters Pictures Archive

66 VeriChip/Carline Jean/KRT

69 Dr. Demetrius Lopes/Dr. Demetrius Lopes/Chicago Institute of Neurosurgery and Neuroresearch

Color Insert

(1) Roboroach/Reuters Pictures Archive; Tooth Implant/Courtesy National Museum of Science & Industry; RadioPaper/Courtesy International Machines Corporation; Background/Ablestock

(2–3) Titan Arum, Nepenthes Plant, Castor Bean Seeds/Robert L. Allen/BugBob; Tree Nettle/© Mike Dodd; Castor Bean Plant/© Educational Images Ltd.; Durian/© Isabelle Rosenbaum/PhotoAlto/PictureQuest; Background/Ablestock

(4–5) Horseshoe Crabs/Jonathan Barth/Getty; Remote Surgery/Spencer Platt/Getty; Dr. Demetrius Lopes/Dr. Demetrius Lopes/Chicago Institute of Neurosurgery and Neuroresearch; Video-camera Pill/Reuters Pictures Archive; Komodo Dragon/Educational Images Ltd./Background/Ablestock

(6–7) Shoemaker-Levy-9 Series/Tom Herbst, Max-Planck-Institut fuer Astronomie, Heidelberg, Doug Hamilton, Max-Planck-Institute fuer Kernphysik, Hermann Boehnhardt, Universitaets-Sternewarte, Muenchen, and Jose Luis Ortiz Moreno, Instituto de Astrofisica de Andalucia, Granada; All Other Images/Courtesy of NASA

(8) Gecko/Reuters Pictures Archive; Cat/PhotoDisc; Cow/Eyewire

Cover

Main image: Ablestock; © Image Ideas, Inc./PictureQuest; Circles: Spiderbot/Courtesy of NASA; Tooth Implant/Courtesy National Museum of Science & Industry; Hand with DNA/PhotoDisc Green

Ripley's Believe It or Not!

Don't miss these other exciting books . . .

World's Weirdest Critters

Creepy Stuff

Odd-inary People

Amazing Escapes

World's Weirdest Gadgets

Bizarre Bugs

Blasts from the Past

Awesome Animals

If you enjoyed **Weird Science**, get ready for

 **X-traordinary X-tremes!**

From extreme sports to extreme creations, you'll find there are no limits to human daring. Read about . . .

Elaine Davidson, who has 720 body piercings, 192 of them on her face

Jon Fabre, who decorated a ceiling in The Royal Palace in Belgium with the wing cases of a million beetles

Meghan Heaney-Grier, who can dive 165 feet deep—without using any diving equipment

Robert Gallup, who was dropped out of a plane while chained inside a mailbag locked inside a cage—and escaped in time to open his parachute and land safely

These are just a few of the incredible people you'll find in **X-traordinary X-tremes!** Who knows? Maybe someday you'll dare to test your limits and discover that you're braver and more unbelievable than you thought!